147 PRACTICAL TIPS
for teaching professors

compiled & edited by
ROBERT MAGNAN

MAGNA PUBLICATIONS, INC.
Madison, Wisconsin

147 PRACTICAL TIPS
FOR TEACHING PROFESSORS
Compiled and Edited by Robert Magnan

©1990 Magna Publications, Inc.

Magna Publications, Inc.
2718 Dryden Drive
Madison, WI 53704-3086
Revised edition. First printing.

Design by Lowell W. Munz

Library of Congress Cataloging-in-Publication Data
Magnan, Robert,
        147 practical tips for teaching professors / compiled and edited by Bob Magnan.
        p.   cm.
    ISBN 0-912150-09-2 : $12.50
    1. College teaching—United States.
I. Title. II. Title: One hundred forty-seven practical tips for teaching professors.
LB2331.M345   1992
378.1'25—dc20
                                                        92-9593
                                                        CIP

Preface

From the pages of *The Teaching Professor*, from the experiences of teaching professors near and far, come these 147 tips for you.

Most of these ideas and techniques were gathered from *The Teaching Professor*. A few come from classroom experiences of other teachers. Some are straightforward suggestions, while others are accompanied by commentaries.

They come with no guarantees. As you know only too well, what works in one situation may flop in another.

So we offer these 147 tips with that understanding. And with the hope that you'll experiment, customize, and personalize.

As always, the essential question is "What works for you?" Some of you will find a lot of new ideas in these pages. Others will pick up only a few — but maybe a few that will make a big difference in your teaching.

We hope that you find something of value in these pages — and we encourage you to try out some of our 147 tips!

Contents

Before You Begin

Teachers have six different identities, according to the expectations of their students. Decide how you want to accept each of these identities — then act accordingly.

1. Be the expert.

You are in the classroom because of your knowledge of the subject matter, your experience and wisdom. That does not imply you know it all, only that you know more than your students. Students expect expertise. But they are also realistic — and perceptive. If you can't answer a question, admit it, then find out.

2. Be the formal authority.

Structure the course. Set standards, goals, and deadlines. Control classroom procedure and behavior. The balance of power is not equitably distributed in the teacher-student relationship. You have to provide form and structure for the learning experience.

3. Be a socializing agent.

You are a representative of your field, and especially of the values, assumptions, and intellectual style that characterize that particular "micro-society." "Socialize" your students to the norms, standards, procedures, activities, and interests of your field. Sometimes we become so immersed in academe we forget we represent the non-academic world. Our students see us as more than just teachers — we're biochemists, anthropologists, businesspeople, architects, lawyers, linguists, engineers ... .

4. Be a facilitator.

Listen to your students. Question them. Pay attention to their needs and interests. Sometimes we suffer from tunnel vision: our students enter our courses without appropriate preparation and skills. They can't use the library properly. They can't organize adequately. They write poorly. They're weak in reading. They can't analyze. We think, "It's not my *job.*" Think rather, "They're my *students.*" Help them, direct them to resources, give them suggestions and guidance, challenge them to develop. That's our job as facilitators.

5. Be an ego ideal.

Students consider teachers as role models, for better or for worse. We may not accept this identity willingly, but since teaching is fundamentally a personal activity, our personality has a direct — and sometimes crucial — influence on the outcome. Stereotypes abound: absent-minded professors, mad scientists, litigious lawyers, airhead philosophers, bottom-line businesspeople … . These are images, not people. And they're negative, not positive. We aren't like that at all, are we? Let your character, your individuality show through your teaching.

6. Be a person.

Students expect teachers to be human. Although we function as teachers and students, we are not "teaching machines" and "learning machines" — we all have feelings and experiences. Be human — in class and outside. Inspire trust in your students. Encourage them to express their ideas and opinions and feelings freely. Sure, sometimes being human is not as efficient as being a machine. But then, sometimes a moment "off the track" can enhance learning more effectively than a long lecture.

Class Organization

7. Organize in terms of people as well as things.

In preparing our courses we choose content units and sequence them appropriately, often according to larger organizing principles characteristic of our discipline. This is organization in terms of *things*, our input — *what* we *teach*. We must also organize in terms of *people*, our output — *how* we *reach*. Consider the cognitive processes and backgrounds of your students. This point is obvious, but often neglected.

8. Work with your students as a team.

We may be perfectly organized, yet our students have trouble following us. Or we may enter the classroom still trying to put it all together, and emerge triumphant, knowing our students were with us all the way. Strange? Not really. Often our feeling of organization actually undermines our progress. Two different worlds: we *create* organization through *preparation*, but our students *perceive* organization through *communication*. Show your game plan!

9. Start class by telling your students where you're going.

Give them a preview, a sort of map. Some teachers like to write the main points of their outline on the board, off to the side. Sometimes, especially when we feel really organized, we forget our students cannot sense this organization. A preview may not be necessary if you give your students a detailed syllabus and you follow it scrupulously. But remember: the best leaders are not always those with the best plans, but those who best communicate their plans.

10. Break to tell your students where you are.

When you plan your class, mark "milestones" and "turns" on your map. When you reach each of these checkpoints, stop — to recap, to question, to establish connections, to answer questions, to indicate any shift in direction.

11. End class by telling your students where you've been.

Toward the end of class, take a moment to summarize the main points of your lecture, then ask if there are any questions. Many teachers neglect to summarize, often for lack of time, then get tangled up in questions that arise because students have trouble following the trail. It's easier for students to formulate their questions if they have a good and fresh overview of the lecture.

12. Keep in touch with the big picture.

Sometimes we lose perspective: what is for us a structured, comprehensive, and interesting treatment of the subject may be for our students a hodgepodge of facts and figures, odds and ends, stretching from bell to bell. In other words, they can't see the forest for the trees. So for every elm or cluster of maples you present, take a moment to connect the part to the whole, to consider relationships, relative importance, cause-and-effect. If you've got reasons for talking about something, make sure your students understand those reasons. If not ... .

The First Day

13. Play "Meet Your Teacher."

Begin the semester by introducing yourself and getting the students to ask questions. "Yeah, it sounds great, but I've tried it already: I hand out information about the course, they read it while I'm going over the details, and there are hardly ever any questions."

How about a slightly different approach? Distribute the syllabus and other handouts and give them time to read everything through. Then divide them into groups, tell them to decide together on questions to ask you and to select a representative to interview you.

The size of the groups depends on the number of students in your class and on group psychology: if the group is too large, certain students will dominate and others won't participate. Optimum might be between three and five. You may decide not to ask them to select a representative until after you've given them time to propose and discuss questions, since sometimes the "representative" takes or is given too much control.

Allow the students free rein in their questions, to ask anything that might inform them about the class or the teacher, whether professional or personal.

Of course, many of the questions will be about the obvious — grading, expectations, assignments, attendance. And there may well be more questions than usual: students are generally more likely to ask questions when they know that they are not asking for themselves alone. Take note: you may want to revise your handouts if things are not clear enough.

Other questions may be less obvious but of greater importance: What are your qualifications to teach this course? What experience do you have outside of teaching? What do you like or dislike about this course? Why did you become a college teacher? What else are you interested in? Don't hesitate to be human: a great advantage of the interview over handouts is to allow you to interact in a personal way. And don't be surprised to find your students are more human too. Express yourself openly and frankly; answer their questions fully but not in excess. And remember to let them guide the interview.

After the interview you may even want to ask questions about this way of beginning the course. How do they feel? What are the advantages and disadvantages? They may be reluctant to assume control. They may enjoy the power of actively getting information. They may like the opportunity to indulge their curiosity. They may feel less awkward about expressing opinions and relating personal experiences. Try it: the experience is certainly worth the time and effort!

At The Bell:
1, 2, 3, Go!

When class begins, you're ready, because this is your life. How about your students? Some have barely arrived from another class, maybe from an exam or from an exciting discussion or from a boring lecture. Others are chatting or reading a newspaper or doing homework.

There's no button to push to make all their minds come to order and get onto the right track when the bell rings. Many teachers don't even try: they simply begin, hoping the material will serve as the catalyst for the miraculous transformation of a swarm of minds into one lean, mean learning machine. But the machine runs better if started with care. Just three or four minutes can make a big difference.

14. Prime your students.

Remind them of what was covered in the previous class, particularly during the final minutes, when minds may have already begun to wander. Remind them of the reasons for covering the material — importance and relevance of certain points, necessity of laying foundation, or whatever.

15. Verify mental operations.

After a few words to start things off, get them involved. Ask a few questions. Or let them fill in the blanks: "Last Friday we were talking about Impressionism and the innovations of _____. Specifically, the most influential aspect was _____."

Just be sure that your framework is specific enough to elicit the answer: a lead such as "In our last class we talked about _____" generally leads only to frustration for teacher and students. And avoid multiple answers with this indirect approach. If you say "The Central Powers in World War I were _____, _____, _____, and _____," you're likely to be hit by a fusillade of answers or — more likely — by confused silence, especially as the lead is vague: you could be asking for names (how many?), adjectives or maybe a verb. Be more direct: "Name one of the Central Powers in World War I. OK, now another? How about one more? And the fourth?"

16. Whet their appetites.

After you prime and verify, *push!* Ask questions to lead them from the review to material you'll cover next. Get them to wonder: use questions such as "What about ..." or "What happens if ..." or "How would it be ..." to stimulate them, focus their attention.

Physicality

DELIVERY

We are surrounded by ink and paper, written language.
It's not surprising we have trouble conveying material in class.
When we translate facts and ideas from page to stage, there are a
few things to remember.

17. Pace your delivery to your material.

It's a simple idea, but often neglected, particularly because
teachers get involved in their subjects. You've probably given your
material a fair amount of thought: don't your students deserve that
same opportunity?

18. Think through your ears.

Written language is generally more compact, more involved,
than speech. Written language relies on discrete signals: single ideas
exist in statements that form sentences, groups of ideas are gathered into paragraphs. When we speak, we need other signals.
Listen to professional speakers — TV and radio newscasters,
actors, preachers: How do they put impact into their words?

19. Pause to punctuate.

All speakers pause to breathe; good speakers pause to punctuate.
Pause slightly at significant points — after each item in a list, after
a key word or phrase, after an important sentence, after quoting

someone. Use a lengthy pause to signal a change of thought — the oral equivalent of a paragraph: move to another location, erase the board, consult your notes, or ask if there are any questions.

20. Match your music with your lyrics.

Effective speaking is like a song: even the best words will suffer without proper delivery and intonation. It's not difficult to do justice to your material. You don't need great oratorical skills or carnival barker gimmicks.

When we want to emphasize something, it's natural to turn up the volume. But it's sometimes effective to lower the volume, even to a conspiratorial whisper. When you signal a conclusion with "And finally ..." or "To sum it all up" or similar wording, use intonation to underline this shift and insert more frequent, shorter pauses.

21. Don't forget the spice.

How often have we heard that variety is the spice of life? And how often do we think only in terms of matching delivery with material? Sometimes what's appropriate for three minutes may not work for seven. Switch to another delivery — a different tone, a different phrasing — just for variety. In baseball terms, it's not the *pitch* itself as much as the *change of pace.*

22. Take chances.

No rules of syntax dictate these directional cues. Our use of cues is less precise than our use of written signals, so we may be less successful on one occasion, but more effective on another. If we accept this fact, we can appreciate classroom delivery as an *art,* a chance to be free to *experiment.*

MOVEMENT

23. Think physical.

So often in class the mind moves about unaware of the body. Some teachers tend to pace as they lecture, because they are nervous or excited. Or they may move their hands around a lot, for the same reasons. Others stand still, often behind a lectern or desk, their hands clutching their notes or stuck in their pockets or dangling lifeless at their sides. How about you? What is your body doing while you lecture?

24. Get a second opinion.

Ask a colleague to observe your movements. Find out if your limbs are out of sync with your words and your material.

25. Practice your delivery.

Use a confined area if you tend to pace, a large room if you generally stand still. Pay particular attention to your hands: concentrate on meaningful movement.

26. Put on a mask.

We can learn a lot through playing roles. If you move your hands constantly, imagine you're a funeral director. If you have dead hands or robotic gestures, imagine being a fire-and-brimstone preacher. *Play with it!*

27. Go theatrical.

Insert instructions in your notes, as if you were a director working with an actor: "Don't pace!" or "Hit desk for emphasis!" or "Walk to side of room!" or "Stop and write this part on board." This may seem odd, but think: if you work hard preparing your class, choosing facts and terms and other details to include in your notes, why not jot down a few more words as a sort of "insurance policy" for all your work?

28. Use spatial expression.

Suppose you often find yourself digressing, to clarify a point or to change mood or direction or to hit an interesting sidelight. Why not deliver your tangential comments from a different location? Think of your change of position as choreographic parentheses. If you have a flair for the dramatic, go one step further, changing voices or affecting accents to express different perspectives.

29. Give your students a pause button.

Establish a signal so your students can call a *time-out* — maybe a hand up or "Time out!" What happens? You stop talking. Why? Because they can't take notes fast enough. Because they want you to repeat something. Because they have questions. Because they need a moment to consider a point. But maybe the best reason is to allow them a means of control. Think about it: when we read, we stop — maybe to read something a second time, to weigh a thought, to verify a detail. Time-outs encourage students and teachers to think about the material, to interact, to integrate, to assimilate.

30. Never check with Father Time.

Every time you turn to glance at the clock or move your arm to consult your watch, you acknowledge the authority of time. Be discreet. Check the clock on the wall naturally, as you gaze about the room. Place your watch on the desk or lectern beside your notes. Don't let time intrude on your class.

BLACKBOARDS

Work the boards wisely. The blackboard is indispensable in most classrooms, and we tend to forget we're using it. But it can also intrude upon our material and turn us against our students. A few simple bits of advice:

31. Erase the entire board when you enter the room.

This is a great way to establish your presence. Remove all traces of whatever subject occupied the room previously. Many teachers then put the homework assignment on the board — off to the side, generally as close as possible to the door. This is practical, but also psychological: you establish your presence.

32. Erase the entire board after each main section.

This activity has several advantages:

- You signal the end of a section in a physical way,
- You allow a short pause for reflection or recuperation,
- You create space to summarize key points and emphasize your answers to any questions,
- You don't leave scattered words and phrases to distract your students,
- You're less likely to need to interrupt the next section to erase.

If you intend to continue immediately into the next section or if you erase after answering questions, you can profit from the brief moment of erasing to shift your mind to the next section.

33. Avoid "patchworking."

Sometimes we're caught up in an important matter and the board is covered. So we erase a small area, write a few words, erase another small area, write some more. And all these pauses and movements tend to fragment our material, especially if our trail of chalk wanders around across the board. If you get caught short of space, simply announce "Time out!" and erase an area large enough for your needs. But there are occasions when the comedic effect of "patch-working" lets you stress a point or add a pinch of variety.

34. Don't get caught between board and material.

If you need to write a few lines on the board, don't pause in the middle of a sentence; finish your thought, then stop to write.

Yes, most of us can write and talk at the same time — but your delivery may lack impact, especially if your voice is directed against the board rather than toward the class. It's usually best to concentrate on one thing at a time.

35. Don't get caught between board and class.

Some teachers ask if there are any questions, just as they turn their backs to erase the board or to write. True, it may allow students a chance to gather their thoughts, but it may also suggest you want to get on to the next matter immediately. And if you get a question, erase before starting your answer (a nice moment to reflect) or after finishing — but not in the middle of your answer. If the question is so complicated you need to use the board, then erase before plunging into the answer. If you find yourself in trouble in midstream, call a time-out to erase. Then time your writing judiciously, so you aren't *talking* and *chalking* at the same time.

Lecturing As Performance Art

Many of us are uncomfortable with the notion that effective lecturing is a performance. We have two main objections: Teachers transfer knowledge and train minds; we should simply present facts and demonstrate mental processes. Teachers are not entertainers; even those of us who can tell jokes or do voices cannot possibly compete with the worlds of stage, screen, television, and the recording industry. But the original meaning of "perform" was to "complete." "Performing" may be simply adding to the transfer of knowledge and the training of minds, something personal, to inspire and excite students, to complete our efforts.

36. Think of it as "show" business.

Many lectures suffer from too much *tell* and not enough *show*. How do you feel when you discover a new fact or encounter a new concept or find a new approach? Well, allow that feeling to *show* in your lectures — be excited about what you're doing!

Any suggestions on enhancing your performance? A few to get you started.

37. Play Q and A.

When you lecture, are you simply telling things? Why not occasionally frame a lecture as a series of questions and answers? It provides an ideal opportunity to develop thinking skills as well: you can use questions to enter into explanations or elaborations, to force a critical analysis, to change direction, to allow meaningful and/or interesting digressions — the possibilities are enormous!

38. Talk it out from dot to dot.

Some constructs or interpretations are difficult to grasp because they consist of so many ideas or facts or steps. It's like working a dot-to-dot puzzle: we understand the picture from the start, so it may be hard to appreciate the situation as perceived by our students. Play the stereotypical egghead prof, scratching your head and puzzling out each step out loud: "OK, how?" and "But why?" and "Then what?" Use the board to map out your course as you go. Just remember to keep your diagrams simple.

39. People your ideas.

Where do you get the ideas you present in your lectures? From Pasteur or Spinoza or Sartre or Euclid or Michelet or Dostoevski … So, put the words back into their mouths.

OK, maybe you don't do voices. Tell stories, then, "live and in person." Try something like, "The year: 1665, the place: England, and a scientist named Isaac Newton is watching the moon and wondering … ."

When you present differing opinions, why not have the proponents argue among themselves or hold a panel discussion? Distinguish between characters through voices or accents, or with hats, or merely by changing position or standing beneath names written across the board.

That's *performing*. The idea is basic: life dries out when it's brought into the classroom. We should allow it to live as much as possible. Just return with your students to the people and places and times that gave us the knowledge we want to transfer.

40. Market your apples.

Ah, the fruit of knowledge! Students should be eager consumers of something so healthy and delicious. So would it hurt to do a little marketing from time to time? Sell those ideas! Make your students want to learn, not just collect grades and credits.

A colleague tells me that when she feels too tired to teach, she plays a little game. She imagines she's teaching on a street corner with an empty hat on the ground. The students are free to wander away or to toss a coin into her hat. She then puts everything she's got into selling her apples of knowledge. She enjoys teaching, but when her energy is low, this sink-or-swim marketing angle keeps her students from catching her case of the blahs.

Teaching Your Students To Think

A recent national poll shows that 52% of Americans believe our schools do an adequate job teaching basic facts and skills, but only 39% are satisfied with their results in teaching to think and reason.

Stretch their heads, don't just stuff them. Create situations that encourage your students to evaluate, to solve problems, to make decisions. Remember the story problems from third grade? College teachers should profit more fully from various possibilities: cases and matters of ethics in business courses, everyday scenes in foreign languages, hypotheticals in law, role-play situations in the social sciences.

If you can't think of problems to solve, maybe you can brainstorm with colleagues — in your discipline or others — or consider opportunities in your community or articles in newspapers and magazines. The world is full of story problems! And if you can't figure out how to teach problem-solving, maybe that problem could be the first subject to toss out to your students!

Think about the types of questions you ask: Are you asking for facts and figures, a simple regurgitation of information? Are you dealing with ideas and concepts in abstraction? Use specifics, and force your students to react.

EXPAND AND EXPLORE

41. Ask for evaluations.

Formulate questions that require your students to apply standards in order to make value judgments. And the key question is "Why?"

42. Ask for inferences.

Set up specific situations to work with deduction and induction. Get them to apply ideas, concepts, rules, or principles to a particular case. Give them a series of examples and have them form generalizations.

43. Ask for causes and effects.

Questions of this sort can be formulated to explore relationships between events and persons, ideas or other events. "Why did Japan attack Pearl Harbor?" "What were the results of the Baroque style?"

44. Ask for comparisons and examples.

Comparisons result from an ability to perceive similarities and differences. "What is the difference between a mussel and a clam?" "How are Judaism and Islam similar?" "Kierkegaard, Kant, and Hegel: Which two are most similar? Which two show the greatest differences?" Challenge your students to examine relationships and to establish links.

45. Ask for solutions.

Problem-solving provides great opportunities to use knowledge, sometimes creatively. "How can we prove these two paintings are the work of the same artist?" "How can XYZ, Inc., prevent takeover by Bigg Bux Holding Company?" "We're the kings of Europe in the fourteenth century: How do we deal with the Black Death?"

46. Wave a red flag.

Include in your lecture a statement or conclusion that contradicts something in the reading material assigned for that class period. This contradiction should wave a red flag for your students. Because the clinker is hidden in your presentation, students are encouraged to pay attention and to analyze. At the end of class, give them three minutes to take this simple quiz: (1) "What was the most important thing you learned or we discussed in class today?" and (2) "Where did you find a Red Flag?" You may want to give extra credit for right answers. But remember: it's not only *what* they discover, but *how*. Start the next class period by listing the flags found, for students to discuss, applying techniques of critical analysis.

P.S. When you encourage students to analyze, they may find mistakes that you didn't intend.

47. Toss them a red herring.

When a class responds well to red flags, try a red herring — "a true statement that, without the application of critical thinking, may initially appear to be false." You can use this herring in place of a flag, or add it as a third question.

In his book, *Teaching Thinking Across the Curriculum*, Vincent Ryan Ruggiero recommends a five-step approach, to combine creative and critical thinking, apply to both problem-solving and issue analysis, and develop the attitudes and dispositions associated with effective thinking.

48. Challenge your students to explore.

Stimulate their sense of wonder. Too often we present information, then ask for it. Try starting with *questions* rather than *answers*. Use their curiosity to develop attitudes and approaches that are *proactive*, not *reactive*. A science teacher advises his colleagues to leave the fundamentals aside for a while and concentrate on things unknown: "Let it be known, early on, that there are deep mysteries and profound paradoxes." Good advice for all of us!

49. Push them to consider and communicate.

Many people settle for expressing a problem as it first occurs to them. When you give your students a problem, push them to examine it carefully, analyze all factors, then put it clearly and concisely into words. What are the facts?

50. Guide them through stages of investigation.

Emphasize through practice the three stages:

- They apply their knowledge to the problem,
- They decide what other knowledge is necessary, and
- They figure out how to access this knowledge.

51. Encourage ideas.

Research shows poverty of ideas is a more serious deficiency than faulty reasoning. Stimulate your students to generate ideas, to explore all possibilities. Make sure they examine the matter from all angles. Too often we choose between *logic* and *intuition*, between left-brain and right-brain: two brains are better than one, two approaches together are more effective than either alone.

52. Help them evaluate and refine their ideas.

They need to choose the best ideas, then make them even better. Make them pursue their solution to the end. How do they plan to implement their solution? Push for details. What difficulties might arise? How can they overcome these complications?

Examples

When in doubt, toss one out. We've all been there: We get tangled or lost in explanations, then we pause, to continue, "For example ... ." We all intuitively appreciate the value of a good example. But sometimes they don't come easily. Suggestions from "Heuristics for Creating Examples" by Stephen Yelon and Michael Massa (*Performance and Instruction*, October 1987):

53. Make them accurate.

Quite simply, your examples should fit the idea to be taught and the purpose of the lesson.

54. Make them clear.

Your examples should be simple and concrete, and use vocabulary and ideas familiar to the students.

55. Make them interesting.

Your examples should relate to experiences and interests of your students. They should also be credible and realistic, although this is secondary. In fact, many teachers are more successful with whimsical or outlandish examples.

56. Make them transferable.

If you use several examples, they should range from easy to difficult, elucidate connections between concept and application, and cover a variety of possible experiences.

Helping Your Students Read

An essential part of helping students learn to think critically involves helping them develop reading skills that enable them to analyze, interpret, evaluate, and apply what they read. Many of our students either get lost in the words or remain at the surface. They seek out facts and figures and terms, but they miss out on the inter-relationships and importance of the pieces.

The usual approach to readings is: assign, then question. But the best way to help our students is from the start, before they read.

57. Use a review to preview.

Review facts your students may already know that relate to the reading. This is especially helpful with texts that cover unfamiliar areas or that are heavily interpretive.

58. Give them a bird's-eye view.

Discuss the topic covered in the reading, in general terms. You should provide an overview, but avoid specifics: students should feel the reading is *essential*, not just a *review*.

59. Work with the words.

Go over vocabulary essential to the reading. All words are not cre-ated equal — treat them accordingly: maybe a definition, possibly examples, sometimes a consideration of related terms and concepts.

60. Put questions in their heads.

Questions to stimulate their curiosity. Questions to give them a focus. Give them a mix of general and specific questions: require them to find facts, but also to analyze and evaluate. Be careful about having questions follow the order and/or the wording of the text: this may be very helpful for difficult readings, but it also encourages students to skim for words and phrases, not necessarily meaning. If you lead a discussion, end with several questions.

61. Put questions in their hands.

Give them a guide to follow as they read. You may want to have them write out answers. Some of the questions may ask for facts, but these should be followed by questions requiring interpretation, analysis, and evaluation.

62. Map out a discussion.

Tell them to prepare for a discussion of the reading and give them an outline of the points you'll cover. Leave wide margins to allow for any notes they might want to make while reading.

63. Reverse roles.

Tell them to read as *teachers*. Have them outline the main ideas or lines of the reading and formulate questions to cover these points. Then, choose individuals to lead the discussion for each section of the reading. After each phase of discussion, ask if there are any questions from the class not yet considered.

Large Lectures

STUDENT INPUT

We feel overwhelmed by a large lecture class, a sea of faces. We do our best to reach each and every student — but how do we know what's happening out there? Maybe someone asks a question from time to time. But how many questions remain unasked? And what areas of interest go unexplored?

64. Put out an Odds 'n' Ends Box.

Just set out by the door a box for feedback — questions, thoughts, suggestions, ideas, opinions, commentaries, critiques, or whatever. Encourage your students to contribute. Maybe they're reluctant to speak out, maybe time prevented a question or comment, maybe the idea didn't seem relevant enough.

65. React to their contributions.

Try to begin or end your lectures with items from the box. Integrate their comments into your lectures. Use their questions for recaps. If you accumulate a good number, have an "Odds 'n' Ends Day," using the period to answer their questions and develop their ideas. Remember: show them you value their input, and show how "odds and ends" are rarely as insignificant or irrelevant as they might believe.

PREPARATION

Giving a lecture is not easy: We're often caught between the need to be prepared and the desire to be spontaneous. Our students want knowledge, but they also want life.

66. Don't live in the past.

The word "lecture" originally meant "reading." But now good teachers never *read* their material to their students: they *tell* or *report* or *notify* or *announce* or *explain* ... . As you prepare your lecture, think about which verb would best fit each section. You could even write it in the margin, as a reminder.

67. Work in three phases.

Phase I: Prepare the materials, a day or so in advance: assemble notes, check references and quotations, draw diagrams, synthesize, think of examples, and so forth.

Phase II: An hour or two before the lecture, put your main points and support material on large index cards.

Phase III: In the fifteen minutes before your lecture, go through the cards and review.

There are several advantages to this three-phase approach:

- You'll be more involved in your lecture, if only because it takes more mental energy to speak from notes than to read prepared text.
- Students may feel more inclined to ask questions and offer comments than with a "talking book."
- You'll be more open to questions and comments: student input is more a part of the lecture, not an intrusion.
- You'll feel less compelled to finish the lecture, come what may: simply set aside the cards remaining, for use in the next lecture.

68. Keep a guide at hand.

Prepare a "master" card — a general outline of your lecture and indications of what cards might be dropped or added, depending on time and student reaction. It's easier to keep track of the direction and flow of your lecture while you go through the various points and pathways of your notes.

DELIVERY

69. Think big.

From 20 rows back, even a six-foot-tall teacher looks about an inch high. Eye contact is difficult to establish, let alone maintain. Write on the board or an overhead transparency, then go to the last row and read your writing. Control the volume of your voice: you should hit the back without overpowering the front. Practice making your gestures larger than life. And try to move more frequently — it may make a big difference in holding the attention of those in the back.

70. Claim your territory.

Do whatever it takes to establish and maintain your presence in the room. With a remote microphone you enjoy freedom of movement — departments should provide them for all lecture facilities. If a point is essential, deliver it loud and clear from the front. But to elaborate or illustrate those points, move out among your students. Take advantage of these excursions to establish eye contact with students in the outer regions.

71. Hit them before you lose them.

Arrive early and stay near the door. This is a good strategy if you have materials to hand out, but it also allows you to greet students, exchange a few words, answer questions — before individuals become a crowd.

72. Talk it out.

Be as conversational as you can. Your position alone, standing before a large group in a large room, establishes a certain distance. Students are not there for a formal speech. They need *information*, organized coherently and presented comprehensibly, and the *opportunity to interact* with someone who knows and loves the material. So, relax, act naturally, and *talk* with those people.

Discussion

TEACHER PARTICIPATION

Your discussion questions are brilliant, but somehow students are not eager to participate. Why not? Sometimes we can be defeated by our reaction to their responses: student participation depends on teacher participation.

73. Lead, don't drag.

First rule: less is more. We all know the vicious circle: When students hesitate, the teacher talks. When the teacher talks, the students give up. It's like fishing. You use the right bait, then wait. Don't be so eager or anxious you scare them off.

74. Acknowledge contributions.

Let the students know you appreciate their participation. React to *them* as they react to the *subject*.

- Be careful: sometimes a positive response, overdone, can embarrass as much as a negative response.
- Avoid the trap of stock responses: if every contribution is "Good!" or "Excellent!" these words of praise lose their meaning.
- Be specific: "Good thinking!" "Unusual, but you're right." "Well, in a certain sense, yes." "I'm glad you remembered that." "Ah, a point I hadn't considered!"

75. Dig.

Ask for more information, going for what the student knows, not what he doesn't know.

76. Develop.

After acknowledging an answer, take it somewhere: emphasize or elaborate or present another perspective or opinion. Remember: your transition here is crucial.

77. Accept the unexpected.

When a student makes a point, the worst reaction is "No, that's not what I had in mind" or a puzzled look and silence. Classrooms are for learning, even (especially?) for the teacher. React to the *point*, not to your *disappointment*.

78. Follow their lead.

Take their responses and ideas and suggestions and questions and follow them as far as the students find interesting and you consider worthwhile. Don't worry about getting "off the track": a discussion should run on intellectual energy, not straight and narrow rails.

79. Put their input on display.

Jot their responses, suggestions, ideas, questions on the board. Chalk talks, loud and clear. One study on note-taking during lectures reports students recorded 88% of the information on the board, but 52% of the critical ideas were left unwritten. We all know what goes on the board is important — why not something from your *students*?

80. Grade yourself.

Take a moment after every class and give yourself a grade for participation, maybe using the tips suggested above. How open are you to your students? How flexible? How do you encourage them to get involved? How do you deal with wrong answers or irrelevant comments?

STUDENT PARTICIPATION

You present some material — very well, you believe — and then you open up the class for discussion. The students are quiet. You ply them with questions. You pry at their silence. The silence becomes embarrassing, oppressive. If students respond, they do so in bits and pieces, a few words here and there, directed back at you. All eyes are on you or downward. Discussion becomes drudgery. You wonder why you even try.

Sound familiar? Sometimes (often?) classes have to be prepared for discussion. It's not simply a matter of preparing them intellectually, with material: you've got to prepare them psychologically, from the very start.

There are two good exercises that involve tasks' and interaction the first day of class, after you give your introductory spiel. These tasks' may be general, such as "Find two students who are majoring in history" or "Find someone with a nickname" or "Get a name, an address, and a telephone number from four students" or "Find a student who enjoys classical music" or "Find a student who dislikes baseball." Or you may prefer more specific tasks — in an advanced German course, "Get five students to name their favorite German novel" (with all interaction to be in German); in a history course, "Get three students to name five events that had the most impact on shaping the American mentality, in their opinion."

81. Jump start your students.

Have your students stand. Distribute slips of papers or index cards with 'tasks.' You may want to give each person only two or three tasks, with the same task going to several people. Allow them five or ten minutes to accomplish their tasks and to take notes. Then have individuals (don't ask for volunteers) read their 'tasks' and the results to the others. Ask the others for comments or reactions.

82. Run your students around in circles.

This introductory exercise is more structured and better suited for a shorter period. Divide your class into two equal groups; if the number is uneven, you join the smaller group. Form two concentric circles, with each student in the inner circle paired with a student in the outer. Give 'task' slips to students in one

circle and ask them to question their peer in the other circle. If
the arrangement of chairs prevents forming circles, establish 'stations': put members of one group in each corner and at intervals
along the walls, then have the members of the other group visit
these stations.

After a certain length of time, depending on the questions
and the amount of interaction, call out "Circle left!" and have
the circle of questioners rotate to change pairings. For variety
you may want to have the circles rotate by more than one person
or have each student give his slip to his peer before rotating.
Then have your questioners report their results to the others.
Encourage reactions.

Benefits:

- You break the ice, relieve "opening day nerves," push
  your students into action.
- You emphasize class dynamics. Students need to realize
  that being in a class means being with other students, not
  just with a teacher. And sometimes teachers need to be
  reminded that it may be best to set things in motion and
  then step aside.
- You and your students get a general feel of the people
  behind the faces — backgrounds, attitudes, personalities.
  Many students hesitate to ask questions or give answers
  in class because they don't know the others — they are
  afraid of the *unknown*.
- You form a foundation for interactive discussion: stu
  dents exchange questions and answers. You force them to
  get involved, but nobody is on the spot: there are no
  spectators or judges, only participants. When they present the results to the class, there is a spotlight, but there
  is also a feel of empathy from those in their seats, because
  the results are from a shared experience.

Be creative! And remember: the key is to involve all the students from the start, the purpose is to encourage interaction.

CONCEPT AND STRUCTURE

Many good ideas for discussions have been collected in
Classroom Communication, edited by Rose Ann Neff and
Maryellen Weimer. But one crucial yet simple point can be
made here.

83. Dare to develop.

Many teachers tend to structure discussions as if they were linear series of questions and answers in a book. But many students feel greater freedom to participate when they realize it's not necessary to enter into a lockstep of questions and answers. The "star" model may be more productive:

- In preparing, pick a number of fairly distinct topics.
- List questions or ideas relating to each topic, on index cards or separate sheets of paper.
- In class, ask a general question to get into a topic.
- Then follow whatever lines interest your students, using other questions or ideas to develop discussion of that topic.
- Put the topic in the middle of the board and radiate the responses and suggestions in all directions, to help keep track of matters and to represent graphically the natural flow of the discussion.

ODDS AND ENDS

Get a little life into your discussion. Or rather, get out of your discussion and into life. Some ideas:

84. Contact the players.

There's no reason to keep your students immersed in books and newspapers when the people being studied are alive and out there somewhere. Find them — politicians, business leaders, artists, whoever. Have your students discuss and formulate questions. Then, contact the subject — by phone or by letter.

85. Travel through time and space.

"Contact the players? Good idea, unless they're dead." Where there's a will (or at least a grave), there's a way.

You teach history, and your students find it all, well, kind of old. Why not have them interview famous or representative people from the past?

You teach philosophy, and your students get lost in all those words and ideas. Why not have them ask questions of the masters themselves?

You teach literature, and Chaucer and Dickens and Flaubert and Tolstoi just don't make it for your students. Why not have them go straight to the source?

You can play the star role yourself, or you might want to assign roles to students. You can have a single interviewer or a small panel, or the entire class can toss out questions. Remind them to pay attention to authenticity and to point out inconsistencies in the characters or inaccuracies in the facts.

Group Projects

There are several advantages to group work:

- It develops cooperation and planning skills.
- It encourages leadership and active participation.
- It leads to better relationships within the class.
- It prepares students for the real world.

Yet there are inherent difficulties. How can you avoid these pitfalls?

86. Make the task specific and concrete.

Questions about purpose and goals can waste a lot of time.

Make it clear: "Establish five reasons for the Civil War" or "Identify the three most important points in the reading" or "List the information needed to complete the experiment" or "If we suspect achrestic anemia, what test do we run?"

Put it in writing, either on paper or on the board. If the task is involved, suggest they take notes.

Sometimes it's useful to have them keep "minutes":

- They show the progress of the group, which motivates students to keep on task and allows you to see where questions or problems arise.
- They encourage input from each member.
- They allow for "readback." Sometimes students are more likely to contribute when they can do so "in pieces," and less likely to forget what comes to mind. Their contributions are recorded in a list, establishing an agenda. Then each point is read, one by one, to allow for elaboration and reaction. The minutes serve as a map, letting them pursue a line of thought freely, then guiding them back to the main path or other lines.
- They are noted as they happen, requiring no editorial effort.

Since it's difficult to both *record* and *react*, the task of recording can be shared, the notes passing from hand to hand at regular intervals or whenever there is a change of speaker.

87. Match group size to the task.

Some research indicates five is the most personally satisfying number for participants. Groups with five to seven members will probably function most efficiently on class projects. Beyond seven, students feel less opportunity — and pressure — to participate. Short, in-class projects generally are best with only three or four members.

Avoid having the same number of members as tasks: members often naturally assume a division of labor, with each responsible for one task, which may preclude discussion and interaction.

88. Keep time limits tight.

Groups never have enough time — generally because interactive bonds take time to develop and because group problem-solving methods are usually not very efficient. Give your students a clear sense of deadline. Although more time usually means better results, in the "real world" there are often constraints. Announce at regular intervals the time remaining.

89. Do something with their work.

Share the results with the entire class. There are several possibilities, depending on size and time.

- Have each member report on a certain facet: the report may be oral — either immediately or during the following class — or written as homework.
- Ask groups to each select a representative to present their findings.
- Instruct groups to write out a summary of their conclusions or ideas, which you then read to the class.
- If you asked them to keep minutes, collect these and read them to the class, or transfer them to transparencies, for discussion. With minutes there is an important bonus — you can get into *strategies* of problem-solving, as well as *results*.

Remember: nobody likes to spend time and energy on a task only to have nothing happen with the results.

How Are You Teaching?

CHECK WITH YOUR STUDENTS

It's like a report card: we work hard, then get our grades. But why wait until the term is over to evaluate your teaching? Why think too late about what might have been? Why not get feedback earlier, so you can improve? There are several ways.

90. Go casual.

Take a few minutes at the end of class, a few weeks into the semester, for an informal, open discussion about the direction of the class, about what's working and what's not. But remember: students may be reluctant to be candid and speak their minds.

91. Get it in black and white.

Try a more structured approach, such as the Teaching Behaviors Inventory presented in the October 1988 *Teaching Professor* or the laboratory instruction assessment presented in the March 1989 *Teaching Professor* or "Effectively Using Informal Early Semester Feedback" and "Written and Verbal Methods for Early Semester Feedback" (Illinois Instructor Series, *Teaching Professor*, October 1988). The tools vary, but they all have two major advantages: every student participates and they can be totally honest.

92. Open a Suggestion Box.

Get a shoebox, cut a slit in the lid, and mark it as a suggestion box. You can even decorate it — sometimes a whimsical touch puts students more at ease. Tape it to your office door and bring it to class regularly. Just be sure to leave the box unattended: make it a habit to put the box in the room, then go out for a drink of water or a breath of fresh air.

REACTING TO STUDENT EVALUATIONS

The way we react to evaluations is crucial: it determines which path we take — or whether we hit a dead end.

93. Be open.

If you don't want criticism, don't ask for evaluations. Better yet, get out of teaching. Teachers are doubly vulnerable to criticism. We do our work out in the open, before the eyes and ears of our students. And our minds must be open to all means of improvement — for our students, but also for ourselves.

94. Be objective.

Get *outside* the situation. Imagine that the comment is directed at a third person. Consider the evidence on this "other" teacher: Is the comment accurate? How would you react if you were a student in class with this "other"? What would you say to help this teacher?

95. Keep things in perspective.

How many evaluations are there? How many students expressed this criticism? Each student expresses a single opinion: avoid assuming any individual to be speaking for others.

96. React to substance alone, not speculation.

Don't fret over what the student might have meant by this word or that, or if she might be suggesting something else. It's ironic: Some teachers read evaluations more closely than scientific formulas, literary masterpieces or historical documents. This is a great way to lose perspective.

97. Weigh the testimonies.

Sometimes this is simply a numbers game, especially with a larger class or a wide range of abilities and learning styles. Some say "disorganized," while others say "inspired" or "flexible." Some say "directive" and "forceful," while others say "tyrannical." You can only count the votes. This is especially the case when the evaluations consist in part or in whole of numerical scales.

98. Check out the witnesses.

If you receive input from students personally or you can otherwise know the source of the comments, consider the perspective. Some students are exceptionally perceptive and offer excellent insights, while others are very sensitive, easily annoyed or offended.

99. Concentrate on your goals.

Sometimes evaluations are anonymous, with only an indication of the GPA to guide your analysis. Take the grades that represent your "target" — some teachers like to challenge the best students, while others are more concerned about those at high risk — and assess your results in terms of your goals for the course. If you tried especially hard to explain things in the course, comments of "confusing" mean more than "dry." If you aimed at getting and holding their interest, "disorganized" is less important than "boring."

DO IT YOURSELF!

We all worry about our teaching from time to time. This concern is very natural — and it can be very beneficial, if we channel our concern.

100. Lie down on the couch.

Ask yourself probing questions. Why are you teaching this course? What are your goals for your students? In what ways will they be different because of this course? What do you do every class period to promote these developments? What are your goals for yourself? If you are at the midpoint in the semester, are you halfway to your goals? Write down your answers. Be *honest.*

101. Use a high-tech mirror.

Get someone to videotape your class. Then sit down — preferably in a student desk or other less comfortable seat — and observe. Think of it as a TV show, as someone else. Jot down strengths as well as weaknesses. Watch student reactions.

- How much do you talk?
- How much do your students talk? When?
- How much do you move? Why?
- *When* and *what* and *how* do you write on the board?
- How much do students use the board? Why?

Use the pause button to allow time for notes, if necessary, and the reverse, but not too much: it's important to maintain the speed and rhythm of the class.

102. Keep a journal.

No matter how tired or distracted you are at the end of class, take a moment to jot down a few general *impressions* ("I talked too much" or "sluggish discussion") and any *details* that come to mind — great questions, examples, and so forth. Don't hesitate to take notes during class as well. A few words in margin can help you recall for the next class or the next semester any questions, problems, comments or discussion topics. A second or two can be a most worthwhile investment!

Motivating Your Students To Read

How do you get them to read? Sure, there's the "stick approach" — pop quizzes. But that's not a very satisfactory solution. What about using carrots?

103. Give them reasons to read.

Don't repeat in class the material in the readings: this method absolves those who don't read and penalizes through boredom those who do.

104. Assume the best.

This is one area where teachers tend to be pessimists. They assume students aren't reading, then they teach in ways that confirm what they suspect.

Don't ask how many have done the assignment: there is safety and comfort in numbers. Besides, if you know there are some who aren't reading, you feel obliged to summarize for them, don't you?

Avoid trying to cover all the material with your questions: students who haven't prepared will be encouraged to rely on answers from those who've read the material, and it will also be obvious to non-readers how many are not reading.

If the same few keep volunteering answers, stop calling on them: they'll understand. And don't pursue any question for too long: it wastes time, students who are unprepared find safety in numbers, good students become bored or frustrated. Remember: a question left unanswered can sometimes produce valuable results.

Let students feel left out, like they've missed something important. And don't make it less important by skipping over the reading or by lecturing the material. Don't try to make students feel uncomfortable or defensive: missing out on something worthwhile should be sufficient motivation to do the assignment.

105. Use readings in class. And expect resistance.

Talk about the material, but don't review it in detail. Work *from* the text, not *in* it. If students ask questions, cite pages in the book that answer their questions. Give an example or case or read a short quotation and ask students to explain how it fits with the theme or argument of the chapter.

106. Send them on a treasure hunt.

If you're assigning a reading, there must be something valuable in it. Choose several sections or blocks of pages, then ask students to find the most important point, idea, argument, example — whatever — and write it down, together with a brief sentence or two justifying this selection.

If you choose carefully, you can increase understanding and participation immediately. Some students may be able to accomplish this task without reading all the material, but they'll soon tire of this game and resign themselves to reading what's assigned.

107. Find the weak link.

Select a section or passage and ask for the weakest argument, the worst example, the least important point.

108. Turn them loose.

This activity places a greater burden on your students. Don't select any sections to target within the assigned pages. Ask them to choose an argument or philosophy or theory, and write out one or two counterarguments or refutations. Ask them to choose a point and write out several examples. Ask them to take an example and find a few others. Then collect their work or use it as the basis for discussion.

109. Borrow from the pros.

How do people outside our profession market information? Learn from them! Newspapers use headlines to attract attention, sometimes with a touch of sensationalism. Magazines use pull-quotes to draw readers into the text. Movies show clips from coming attractions. TV series use previews to build interest.

Try something a little different. Vary your approach according to the content and situation. Treat your class as if you have to sell them on reading — because we do.

110. Appreciate reading.

This is generally easy, because all teachers enjoy and value reading. But you've got to let that appreciation show: let your students in on experiences you associate with that reading, difficulties you found, things you learned, how it relates to something else in your life — even how you were too busy or too tired to get the most out of it. In other words, be *human*: share *reading* and *reacting* with your students.

Work With Your Colleagues

Students learn better when they can interact. And teachers teach better when they can share their experiences.

Get together with a colleague for one or more of the following activities:

111. Observe each other teach.

112. Talk with students from your colleague's classes.

Serve as an intermediary, to channel feedback about student experiences and reactions to your colleague. Respect their confidentiality, of course. You can also help them resolve minor difficulties, judiciously.

If they have a negative reaction to something, ask them to suggest alternative strategies. If they have a positive comment, pass it along. Then you and your colleague can discuss the good and the bad and strategies for improvement.

113. Review a test from your colleague's course.

Even better, get a student's perspective — take a test. If you're familiar with the content, you can offer suggestions:

- How well does it cover the material?
- Is the coverage balanced?
- Is the structure of the test — essay, short answer, multiple choice, fill-in-the-blanks — appropriate to the material?

Whether or not you're familiar with the content, you can provide input on clarity, scope, organization, length, time required.

114. Complete a set of readings or homework problems.

Then list questions you'd most like to discuss. Teachers tend to become complacent or bored when they've taught the same course a number of times, particularly introductory or basic courses. A new perspective can make a world of difference.

115. Read a book about teaching.

Arrange to discuss a chapter a week. We would recommend *The Craft of Teaching* by Kenneth Eble or *Teaching Tips* by Wilbert McKeachie.

Sometimes teachers benefit more when they get away from the arena. What are the educational implications of *No Contest: The Case Against Competition* by Alfie Kohn or *Pedagogy of the Oppressed* by Paulo Friere or *Winning the Brain Race* by David Kearns and Denis Doyle?

What if you don't have the time or opportunity to read an entire book or to sit down together once a week? How about an article, in one sitting? Choose an article, read it in pieces or alternate reading it aloud, and discuss each section. You may prefer a general or theoretical piece, such as the readings suggested in the June 1988 *Teaching Professor*. Or you might benefit more from an account of some specific experience to be found in a journal in your field — "How I Teach Polynomials" or "A Different Approach to Silas Marner."

116. Review and discuss student evaluations of each other's classes.

Try to interpret in terms of specifics and to translate into positive action. Sometimes we believe our methods and techniques are dictated by our subject matter and by our personalities. A colleague can often provide a different perspective and suggest different approaches.

117. Be professional.

Many of the suggestions for reacting to student evaluations apply when dealing with colleagues. Be open to their comments. Be objective in evaluating your teaching: distinguish between the *person* and the *performance*. Keep things in perspective: we all have imperfections, because we're all human. Get it straight — if you don't understand the comments, ask your colleague to explain.

Then ask for suggestions and alternative strategies. But remember — it's only one person's opinion. And factor your colleague's teaching style and personality into the equation as well.

118. Draw up a plan for improvement.

- *Prioritize.* Consider your goals, for the specific course and for your teaching in general: this sharpens your focus.
- Divide and conquer. Establish *categories* — content, organization, preparation, manner of presentation, class structure, explanations, answering questions, discussion techniques, motivating students, test construction, grading, and so forth. For each category choose one or two problem areas.
- List strategies for improvement — be *specific*.
- Put these strategies into action, *piece by piece*. When preparing your syllabus, refer to the list under "content" and "organization." When preparing each class, check the list for "manner of presentation" and "class structure." When writing out your notes, use the margin to signal strategies — "ask for questions" or "slow down" or "put on board."
- Be *persistent* and *creative*. Some changes are simple. But not all changes are going to work, and surely not easily. Try different approaches.

If you're new at teaching, check with a senior colleague or think back on teachers you had: How do or did they deal with your situation? If you're experienced, it might be helpful to talk with a junior colleague or with a colleague in another area of teaching — anything to get fresh perspectives.

Motivation: Critical Moments

We all go through times when our interest and enthusiasm are low, when we just don't have the energy or the desire to teach effectively. We need a little R and R, but we can't get away.

Here are a few suggestions.

119. Return to reasons.

Sometimes we really can't see the forest for the trees. Spend a few minutes asking students for their reasons *why* they're studying the subject. How about other possible reasons? Don't settle for *intermediate* or *stock* answers. Challenge your students!

"Calculus is required for engineers." Why? What uses are there?

"Arts and Letters requires a foreign language and Spanish is easy." Who says so? Why? Are there other, more practical reasons? What can you do with Spanish? Why require a foreign language?

Don't be surprised if the reasons they give for learning your subject are different from your reasons for teaching it.

120. Check out your own reasons.

Why are you teaching biology or computer science or philosophy? You probably have a knack for your subject — but you certainly aren't teaching it just because it's *easy* for you. You enjoy your field — but that in itself isn't enough. That's the *past*.

Think forward: What are your purposes? And why are you teaching, rather than applying your knowledge and skills in other ways?

Answering these questions can help us situate our efforts within a larger framework, to give us a better perspective and renew our thoughts and energies.

121. Take a class in something new.

Plunge into an area where you're a beginner, where you'll have questions, where you'll need to admit having problems. It's always a good idea for *teachers* to be *learners*, to be broadening their experiences and enhancing their skills. But when we get into something different, we usually do so out of curiosity or for the excitement of learning or to improve in our field or related areas. These are all good reasons, of course. And we generally pursue these lines in our own ways: it's only natural.

But when we take a class, we can expose ourselves to some of the *less enjoyable* aspects of learning — long hours in class, tedious studying, lackluster exercises, asking questions, coping with personality differences, meeting deadlines, taking tests, writing papers or doing projects. Every class is less than enjoyable at some point in some way; every teacher is less than perfect for all students.

Make note of what you like and what you don't like. What works? What doesn't work? Then compare your lists. Look for things that work but you don't like. Chances are you avoid this sort of approach or exercise or technique in your classroom. Consider trying it — not just once, but several times, in several ways.

Evaluating Your Students

GRADING WRITTEN ASSIGNMENTS

122. Interact.

It's easy, especially when grading stacks of essays or a series of routine assignments, to mark mistakes or other negative points and give a grade — nothing more. Sometimes, though, a word or two about something positive might make a big difference in student attitude and behavior. Maybe a marginal note, "Good idea — why not mention this in class?" or "Why do you think so?" or "Yeah, that's something I hadn't considered." Be brief, be sincere, be positive. Like the song says, "Little things mean a lot."

GRADING PARTICIPATION

How often do we tell our students a certain percentage of their grade for the course will be for participation? And how often do we tell them just what we mean by "participation"? And how clear is this area in our own minds? Here are five considerations:

123. Grade on content mastery.

Students should show an understanding of facts, concepts, and theories presented in the course. What are they learning?

124. Grade on communication skills.

Students should ask questions, answer questions or otherwise contribute in a comprehensible manner. How do they express themselves in this area?

125. Grade on interaction.

Students should offer constructive criticism and build on each other's ideas. How do they work with others?

126. Grade on creativity.

Students should use the material to generate other insights and applications. How do they go beyond what is given?

127. Grade on valuing.

Students should identify values inherent to the material and justify according to some value system. How do they find and evaluate what is human within these things?

These five considerations come from teachers. The following were generated by students:

128. Grade on cognitive dimensions.

Consider such aspects as logic, knowledge, and creativity.

129. Grade on expressive aspects.

How clearly do students express themselves? How fluent are they? How concise?

130. Grade on affective ingredients.

We all recognize the important positive effects of enthusiasm and interest. Why not allow some consideration for these aspects of participation?

131. Grade on what student comments contribute to the process of learning.

How do students help each other? Are their reactions relevant? Is their criticism constructive?

GRADING TESTS

132. Bear in mind: absolute means perfect.

We prepare our test, we distribute points, and the rest is simple arithmetic. Our students receive what they earn. We don't get involved in additional mathematical computations and manipulations. Absolute grades are a perfect system. Well, almost.

A perfect system demands perfection. Was your last test perfect? Comprehensive and balanced? A mixture of exercises to suit various cognitive styles? The proper blend of low-discrimination and high-discrimination items? And when you marked the tests, were you careful to apply exactly the same standards to all — and on subjective exercises as well as objective?

133. Be careful on the curves.

Many instructors like the security of grading on the curve: it's reassuring to have a constant distribution of grades, and it's nice to avoid labels of "easy touch" or "hard-nosed."

But there are important disadvantages. When we use curves we may be less critical about our tests: we are certainly compelled to analyze a test when half of our students fail or when most receive A's, but what about when we know in advance how the grades will distribute? And what are the effects of predestination of grades? When the less gifted students feel they'll end up with the lowest grades no matter how they try and improve? When the better students know they're in line for top grades no matter what? When the more ambitious or less scrupulous realize competition precludes cooperation? A 93% earns only a B in one class, while the same grade in another rates an A. And what messages do we send our students when we imply that all their individual abilities and efforts will fit — bottom line — the same bell shape as all other classes?

Reviewing: One More Time ...

How do you review? Or, to put it another way, how do you compress weeks of material into a single class period and how do you find other ways to explain what they didn't understand the first time? Good questions. No wonder many teachers question the value and purposes of exam review sessions.

134. Establish your purposes.

Why are you conducting a review? What is the relative importance of each reason? Structure your review session according to your purposes.

REVIEWS CAN HELP STUDENTS COPE WITH EXAM ANXIETY

135. Draw them a picture.

Give your students a clear and accurate idea of what you'll expect from them. How will they need to demonstrate their knowledge? How detailed should that knowledge be? How will they need to put the pieces together? And, last — but not least — how do you intend to grade their exams? Straight scale? Standard curve? Hybrid? Partial credit for certain items?

Some teachers are unsure about divulging this information. How far should you go? Remember: you can lay out the ground rules without throwing the game. Most students don't want anything more than what is right and fair. Others will push for any advantage. Calm their fears, but don't lull them into a false sense of security. Hold hands, but don't make promises.

REVIEWS CAN HELP MOTIVATE STUDENTS

136. Challenge and cheer.

Make your students work. Make them realize both their weaknesses and their strengths. Give them reasons to be confident and a better understanding of what they need to improve. One colleague compares her review sessions to the pre-game locker room chalk-talk: you're not going to make up for a whole term of classes, you just hope to give them a better sense of themselves and get them pumped up for the big event.

REVIEWS CAN PROVIDE SUMMARY AND PERSPECTIVE

137. Put it in a nutshell.

Give your students an outline, an overview, a way to integrate content chunks. They come in focused on parts — formulas, dates, theorems, definitions, facts. You help them put it all together. This global approach works best in a course where students have taken tests at regular intervals, covering distinct units of material — novels, economic systems, nations of Africa, philosophies, families of plants and animals. In a review you can relate the units, discuss concepts and connections, deal with reasons or attitudes or causes and effects.

138. Keep the ball in their court.

Begin by asking students to name the central theme(s) or concern(s) of the course. Then pursue these lines: force them to identify, to justify their opinions, to compare reactions. Play the devil's advocate. Play the ignorant outsider. Challenge them to think, to decide, to evaluate, to discuss.

139. Put all your heads together.

Many teachers use short answer questions or essays to test their students. Many students dislike these types of exercises because they aren't sure what to put in and what to leave out. An excellent review technique, then, is to toss out a question and then formulate a group response, an entire short answer or the outline of an essay. Students learn a lot from each other. You may assume a passive role, merely a scribal hand to record their work on the board, but you may also need to participate more actively, to challenge and question and stimulate. Remember: organization and ideas and decisions must come from *them*.

REVIEWS CAN FOCUS ON SPECIFIC AREAS OF NEED

140. Apply as needed.

Reviews are like medicine, a remedy for problem areas only. Be prepared to give whatever doses might be necessary. If your students seem to be well-prepared in a certain area, move on to another. If there are weaknesses, concentrate on them.

141. Give your students the reins.

Use the format of open questioning. It's logical: students determine the directions of the review by what they need to know. You place the burden on your students, for better or for worse. Resist the temptation to seize control, to relieve them of their responsibility and freedom. And if their questions end after only five minutes, let the review session end.

REVIEWS CAN AIM
AT SPECIFIC EXAM ITEMS

142. Let them take it for a test drive.

Give your class a "prelim" approach: when you prepare your exam, save the items you decide not to use, then add the instructions from the exam to form a practice test from these extra items, including the percentage or point distribution for each section or exercise. If you can use a computer to create your exams, spinning off a prelim is almost effortless.

Two more advantages: you can test your exercises and you can expose students to your instructions. If an exercise structure is weak, you can improve it. If instructions are unusual or unclear, students can ask questions.

Your prelim should provide a sampling of items. Of course, it's usually best not to take the whole period. The key is "mini-max": minimum time, maximum effect. Then, correct and discuss the items. If there are several possible answers, indicate which are better and why. If there are essays, ask students for the essential points, then evaluate their responses.

REVIEWS CAN PROVIDE FRESH
ANGLES AND APPROACHES

Put a little spin on the ball: try something different.

143. Turn the tables.

Instead of the usual "Teacher questions, students answer," try a reverse. Sometimes this "opposite" approach provides a refreshing change of pace.

144. Host a TV game show.

If you usually ask questions of individual students, form small groups to answer, for your own "College Bowl." Or try a little twist, giving answers and asking for questions, like "Jeopardy."

145. Get a sub.

Designate students, one by one, to stand before the class for a few minutes and answer questions, from the students and from you.

146. Shake it up a little.

Change the physical setting — arrangement of desks, orientation of the room, placement of your desk or lectern. Or just sit down among the students. Sometimes little physical matters assume a great importance over the semester, and small changes can be significant.

147. Invite a guest — yourself.

Play the role of a visitor — a parent, the president of the college, the governor — and have students explain what they're learning — and why. There are lots of possibilities. You've just got to choose something and take a chance.

Final Words

Just as Heraclitus observed that we can't step in the same stream twice, we can't teach the same class twice.

Sometimes our strategies and techniques work wonderfully. And sometimes the same strategies and techniques miss.

We usually search for something different when things don't work. But we should also try other ways when we're successful.

Why? To avoid tunnel vision and norrow tracks and old routines. And so we never forget that we can't teach the same class twice.

Try something different!